HODDER HOME LEARNING

Ment Arithm

UTES A DAY

AGE 7-9

Rhona Whiteford and Jim Fitzsimmons

Illustrated by Sascha Lipscomb

This book provides your child with twenty-eight short activities in mental arithmetic. These are designed to give regular practice throughout the first two years of Key Stage 2, and so the tasks become increasingly challenging as the child works through the book. The mathematics covered in the book reflects the work which he or she will be doing in school. Mathematical symbols (such as – and =) and language (such as **subtract** and **equals**) are explained, and a combination of the two is used. In the same way, children meet numerals (such as **2**) in some questions, and number words (such as **two**) in others.

How to help your child

- Your child should do one Practice Page at a time. It will take most children in this age band about five minutes, but younger ones may need longer. Older or more confident children may be encouraged to complete the page as quickly as possible.
- Provide a quiet place in which to work, to encourage concentration.
- Read the instructions (and the page-by-page hint provided by the squirrel) with your child, and make sure he or she understands the task.
- Your child will probably be able to complete the page independently, but be on hand to help if necessary.
- Encourage neat handwriting and presentation.
- Write the marks for the page in the box, and also on the "totaliser" on page 30. This will give your child a record of progress over time.
- Each page can be used more than once if it is completed in pencil. Scores can then be compared.
- Give positive feedback by writing a brief comment in the speech bubble at the bottom of the page. Phrases such as "Well done!", "Excellent work!" and "Good try!" will help motivate your child.

Hodder Children's Books

NATIONAL CONFEDERATION OF PARENT TEACHER ASSOCIATIONS

The only home learning programme supported by the NCPTA

Practice Page 1

Number/Addition (up to 100)

> This sign means **greater than**.

4 > 2 Four is greater than two.

< This sign means **less than**.

5 < 8 Five is less than eight.

Write the missing sign in each of these.

❶ **13** ☐ **20** ❷ **25** ☐ **18** ❸ **16** ☐ **30**

---

❹ **38 can be written as** ☐ **tens** ☐ **units**

❺ **69 can be written as** ☐ **tens** ☐ **units**

---

❻ Put these numbers in order. Start with the smallest.

24 62 13 33 74 58

☐ ☐ ☐ ☐ ☐ ☐

---

❼ Count on in tens to complete this sequence.

23 33 ☐ ☐ ☐

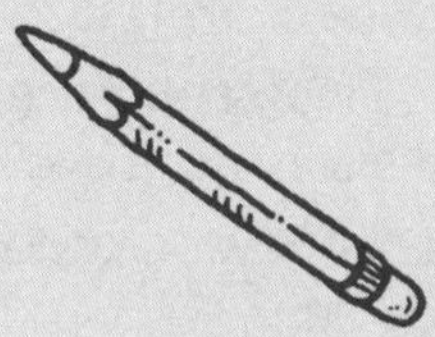

❽ **Increase twenty pencils by sixty pencils.** ☐ **pencils**

❾ **26 more than 3 =** ☐

❿ **Thirty-five plus three equals** ☐

/ 10

Practice Page 2

Subtraction (from numbers up to 100)

1. **19 – ☐ = 15**

2. **Fifty-five minus twenty-five equals ☐**

3. **30 – ☐ = 20**

4. **50 – ☐ = 35**

5. Count back in tens to complete this sequence.

   87 77 ☐ ☐ ☐ ☐

6. **Which number is 30 less than 90? ☐**

7. **Decrease thirty-seven by five. ☐**

8. Count back in fives to complete this sequence.

   35 ☐ ☐ ☐ ☐ ☐ 5

9. **Subtract 70 from 100. ☐**

10. **Kim has thirty-two sweets. How many sweets must she take away to leave sixteen? ☐ sweets**

/10

Practice Page 3 Multiplication

1. 8 x 3 = 3 x ☐

2. 6 + 6 + 6 + 6 + 6 + 6 = ☐

3. What is the product of seven and four? ☐

4. Multiply four by five. ☐

5. 50 x 2 = ☐

6. 20 x ☐ = 80

7. Write in words the number which is double 43.

☐

8. Use the **3x** table to fill in the missing numbers in this sequence.

3 ☐ 9 ☐ ☐ 18 ☐ ☐ 27

9. Which number is five times bigger than ten? ☐

10. Three times greater than eight is ☐

/10

Practice Page 4 Division

1. How many sevens are there in seventy? ☐ sevens

2. How many lots of nine are there in twenty-seven?
   ☐ lots of nine

3. 32 ÷ ☐ = 8

4. Halve six. ☐

5. ☐ ÷ 5 = 4

6. 30 ÷ ☐ = 6

7. Divide twenty-seven marbles equally among nine children.
   How many marbles will each child get? ☐ marbles

8. Which number is one quarter of twelve? ☐

9. What must I divide 24 by to give me equal sets of 3? ☐

10. Share fifty cards equally among ten children.
    How many cards will each child get? ☐ cards

/10

Practice Page 5

2-D shapes/ Measurement

1. Name this shape. 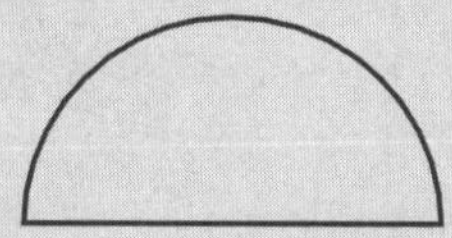

2. Write the name of a 2-D shape with five sides.

3. Write the name of a 2-D shape with six sides.

4. How many sides does a quadrilateral have? sides

5. This is a regular octagon. If one side measures 3 centimetres, what is the distance all the way round? cm

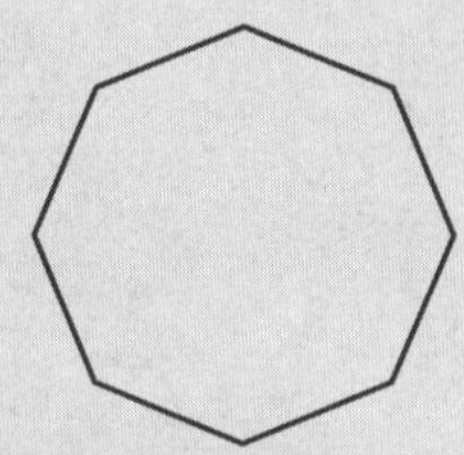

---

6. What is 2 metres 50 centimetres in centimetres? cm

7. Which is longer, 5 metres or 100 centimetres?

8. $\frac{1}{2}$ metre = cm

9. $\frac{1}{2}$ kilogram = g

10. Which is greater, $\frac{1}{2}$ litre or 400 millilitres?

/10

Practice Page 6

Money

❶ 25p + 2p + 2p = ___ p

❷ 10p + 20p + 15p = ___ p

❸ 50p – 20p = ___ p

❹ What is the value of five 20 pence coins? £ ___ . ___ p

❺ What is the value of six 50 pence coins? £ ___ . ___ p

❻ 55p = (___ p) + (___ p) (Use two coins.)

❼ 254p = £ ___ . ___ p

❽ I had 95 pence, but I spent 20 pence.
How much do I have left? ___ p

❾ I had £1.00, and I have 60p left.
How much did I spend? ___ p

❿ Angela has three 5 pence coins and two 10 pence coins.
How much does she have altogether? ___ p

___ /10

Practice Page 7

Time

What time does each of these digital clocks show?

1. 7.00
2. 4.15
3. 6.45
4. 9.30

Write your answers to these as digital times.

5. **15 minutes before 11 o'clock is**
6. **Three-quarters of an hour before 2 o'clock the time is**
7. **Half an hour before 9 o'clock the time is**

8. **How many hours and minutes are there in 68 minutes?** hour minutes
9. **How many minutes are there in 1 hour 15 minutes?** minutes
10. **How many hours are there in 12 half hours?** hours

/10

Practice Page 8

Mixed questions

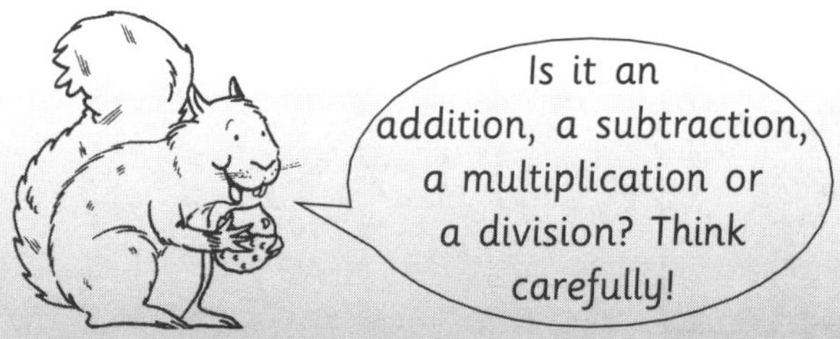

1. 5 + ☐ = 17
2. 15 = ☐ + 5
3. 28 – 5 = ☐
4. 4p x 6 = ☐ p
5. 40p ÷ 4 = ☐ p
6. 80cm ÷ 2 = ☐ cm
7. 60g – 25g = ☐ g

8. Lauren has $1\frac{1}{2}$ metres of fabric, but she needs 4 metres.
How much more fabric will she have to get? ☐ m
9. Ten girls have 50 pence each.
How much money do they have altogether?
£ ☐ . ☐ p
10. If Wednesday is 6th May,
what will the date be five days later? ☐

/10

Practice Page 9

Number/Addition (up to 1,000)

Write the number shown on this abacus.

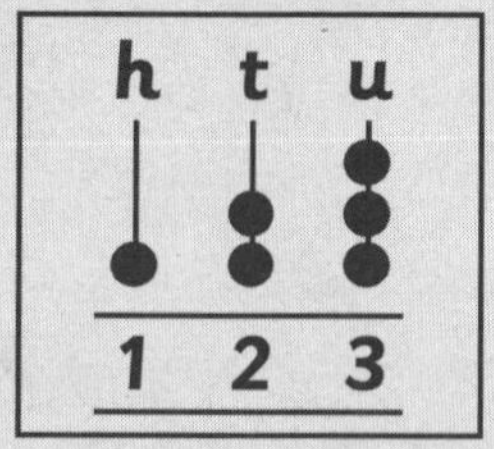

1 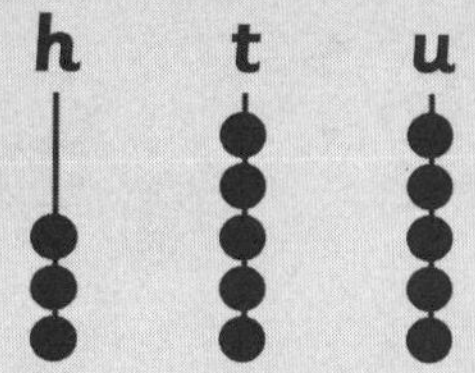

2 What is the value of the 4 in this number?

428

Put these numbers in order. Start with the smallest.

3 **123 321 231 213 132 312**

4 **246 642 462 426 624 264**

Write this number in figures:

5 ***three hundred and fifty-three***

6 Re-arrange these digits to make the largest number possible.

147

---

7 Count on in hundreds to complete this sequence.

125 225 ___ ___ ___ 625

8 **300 + 500 =**

9 **400 + 20 + 3 =**

10 ***Which number is 100 more than 245?***

/10

Practice Page 10

Subtraction (from numbers up to 1,000)

1. What is the difference between 150 and 170? ______

2. Subtract 45 from 460. ______

3. 340 – 8 = ______

4. 500 – 55 = ______

5. There are one hundred and twenty children on a bus.
   If sixty are boys, how many girls are there? ______ girls

6. John had eighty marbles, but he lost twenty-five.
   How many does he have left? ______ marbles

7. ______ – 30 = 150

8. Decrease 100 by 40. ______

9. Thirty less than eighty is ______
   Write your answer as a word.

10. There were ninety sweets in a bag.
    Some of the sweets were eaten, and there were five left.
    How many sweets were eaten? ______ sweets

/10

Practice Page 11

Multiplication

❶ 6 x 4 = ☐

❷ 5 x ☐ = 40

❸ ☐ x 9 = 36

❹ 6 x ☐ = 36

❺ ☐ x 8 = 32

❻ Twenty boys have four books each.
How many books do they have altogether? ☐ books

❼ There are ten stamps in each pack. If Jack buys eleven packs, how many stamps will he have altogether?

☐ stamps

❽ Abbie has twenty soft toys. Emma has three times as many. How many soft toys does Emma have?

☐ soft toys

❾ Charlie has five times as much money as William.
If William has 20 pence, how much does Charlie have?

£ ☐ . ☐ p

❿ Choc Bars are 23 pence each.
How much will two Choc Bars cost? ☐ p

/10

Practice Page 12

Division

Complete these number sentences.

1. 3 x 8 = ☐ ÷ 8 = 3
2. 6 x 5 = ☐ ÷ 6 = 5
3. 5 x 8 = ☐ ÷ 5 = 8
4. 7 x 3 = ☐ ÷ 3 = 7
5. 9 x 4 = ☐ ÷ 4 = 9
6. If I share twenty-four biscuits equally among eight children, how many biscuits will each child get?

   ☐ biscuits
7. A shopkeeper wants to put forty small Easter eggs into packets of ten. She will need ☐ packets.
8. What must I divide 35 by to give me 7? ☐
9. How many fives are there in 75?

   ☐ fives
10. It takes ten links to make a bracelet. How many bracelets can I make from a hundred and twenty links?

    ☐ bracelets

☐ /10

Practice Page 13

Fractions

Half of this shape is shaded.

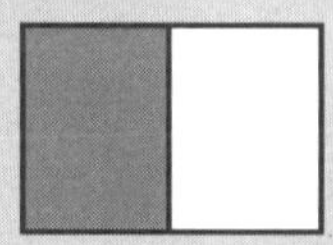

What fraction of each of these shapes is shaded?

1. 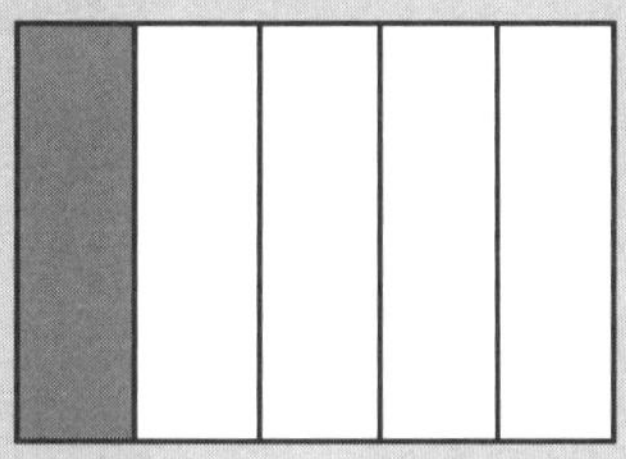

2. 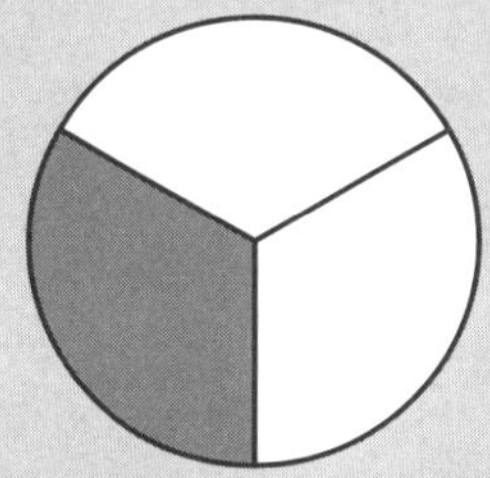

3. 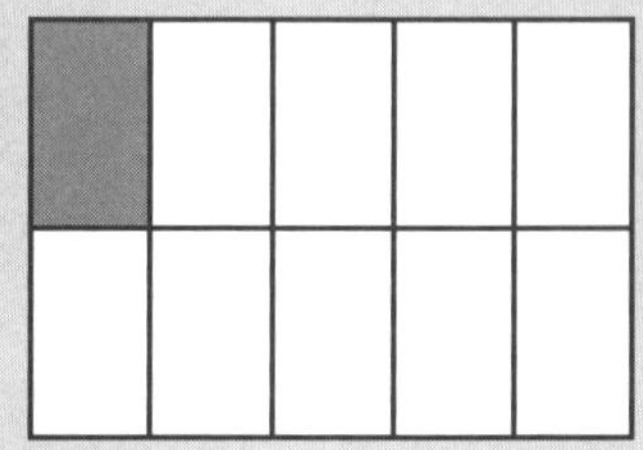

---

4. **How many tenths are there in one whole one?**

   tenths

5. **How many fifths are there in one whole one?**

   fifths

6. **Which number is $\frac{1}{3}$ of 18?**

7. **Which number is $\frac{1}{5}$ of 20?**

8. **Which number is $\frac{1}{10}$ of 40?**

9. **How many centimetres are there in $\frac{1}{10}$ of a metre?**

   cm

10. **How many pence are there in $\frac{1}{5}$ of £1.00?** **p**

/10

Practice Page 14

Money

❶ Five tickets at 10 pence each cost ____ p

❷ Share 25 pence equally among five girls.
How much does each girl get? ____ p

❸ £3.00 – £2.50 = ____ p

❹ What is the difference between
£1.60 and 90 pence? ____ p

❺ How many sweets at 9 pence each can I buy
for 36 pence? ____ sweets

❻ I have one 50p coin and three 10p coins.
How much do I have altogether? ____ p

❼ Take 75 pence from £1.50. ____ p

❽ Pens cost 40 pence each.
How much will five pens cost? £ ____ . ____ p

❾ Share £5.00 equally between ten children.
How much will each child get? ____ p

❿ How many pence are there in £7.83? ____ p

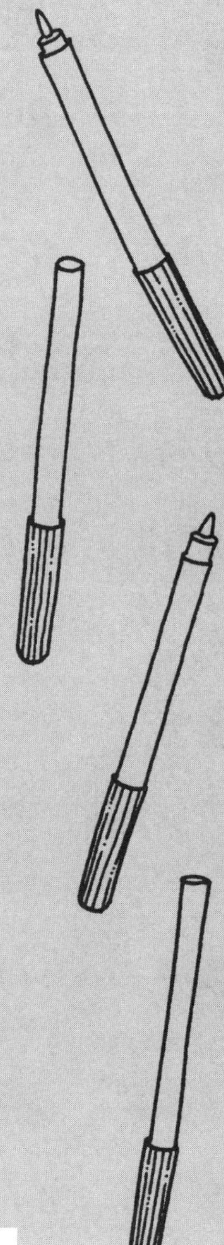

/10

Practice Page 15

Time

What time does each of these digital clocks show?

❶ 10.15

❷ 6.45

❸ 8.35

Write these times as digital times.

❹ **quarter to 3**

❺ **18 minutes past 4**

❻ **20 minutes to 9**

❼ **5 minutes to 1**

❽ **How many minutes are there in $1\frac{1}{4}$ hours?** minutes

❾ **A train leaves London at 5 minutes past 11 and arrives in Guildford at 20 minutes to 12. How long does the journey take?** minutes

❿ **How many hours are there between 10.00 p.m. and 2.00 a.m.?** hours

/10

Practice Page 16

Mixed questions

Write this number in words:

❶ **463**

Write this as a numeral:

❷ ***three hundred and sixteen***

❸ Count back in twos to complete this sequence.

48 46 ☐ ☐ ☐ ☐ 36

❹ **45 ÷ ☐ = 9**

❺ **There are 3 kilograms of potatoes in a sack. The sack is a quarter full. How many kilograms would there be in a full sack? ☐ kg**

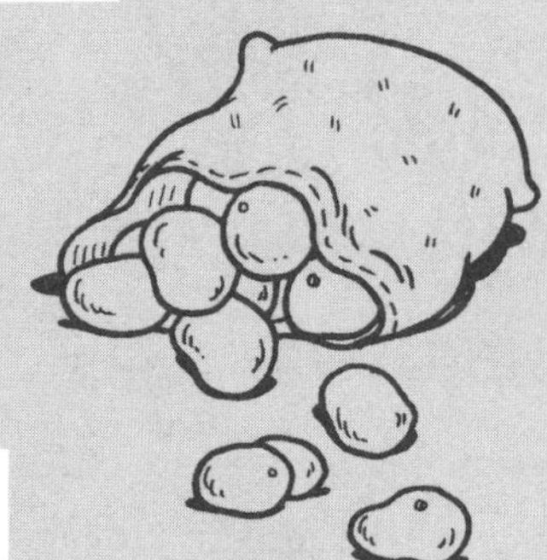

❻ **How many centimetres are there in $2\frac{3}{4}$ metres? ☐ cm**

❼ **Colour $\frac{2}{5}$ of this shape.**

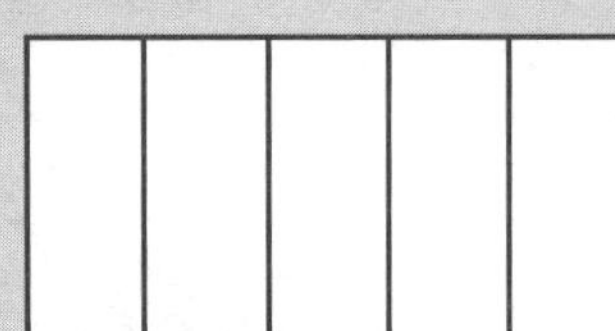

❽ **How many minutes are there in 3 hours? ☐ minutes**

Write this time as a digital time:

❾ **25 minutes to 4**

❿ **What is the product of 20 and 5?**

/10

Practice Page 17

Mixed questions

$$(20 + 20) \div 5 = 40 \div 5 = 8$$

Now try these.

1. $(10 + 20) - 5 =$ ☐
2. $(16 - 8) \times 3 =$ ☐
3. $(3 \times 4) \times 2 =$ ☐
4. $(50 \div 10) + 30 =$ ☐
5. $(20 \div 5) \times 6 =$ ☐
6. $(9 \times 6) - 20 =$ ☐
7. $(50 - 10) \div 4 =$ ☐
8. $(25 + 7) \div 8 =$ ☐
9. $(40 + 40) \div 10 =$ ☐
10. $(100 \div 10) \times 6 =$ ☐

/10

Practice Page 18

Mixed questions

Write this as a numeral:

1. *five hundred and nineteen* [ ]

2. 58 – 35 = [ ]

3. How much more than £1.45 is £1.50? [ ] p

4. $\frac{1}{2}$ of 12 metres is [ ] m

5. 95 + 55 = [ ]

6. What is the total of 24 and 76? [ ]

7. 20 x 5 = [ ]

8. How many half kilograms are there in 3 kilograms? [ ] half kg

9. How many grams are there in 2 kilograms? [ ] g

10. 300 ÷ 10 = [ ]

/10

Practice Page 19

Mixed questions

1. (15 + 30) ÷ 9 = ☐
2. What is the value of the 6 in 362? ☐
3. 120 ÷ 10 = ☐
4. Sam's sunflower is 2 metres 16 centimetres tall, and Shannon's is 8 centimetres taller. How tall is Shannon's sunflower?
   ☐ m ☐ cm
5. Ali has twenty model animals, and Alex has three times as many. How many model animals does Alex have? ☐ model animals
6. If it is 10 minutes past 3, what time will it be in 20 minutes?
   ☐
7. 30 cm + ☐ cm = 1m
8. How many grams are there in $\frac{1}{10}$ of a kilogram? ☐ g
9. How many less than 60 is 20? ☐
10. 300 + 60 + 8 = ☐

/10

Practice Page 20

Mixed questions

❶ How many minutes are there in $\frac{1}{3}$ of an hour?

[ ] minutes

❷ What is the cost of six lollipops at 20 pence each?

£ [ ] . [ ] p

❸ Take 19 from 29. [ ]

❹ [ ] x 8 = 64

❺ (5 x 9) – 15 = [ ]

❻ What number is 100 more than 57? [ ]

❼ 48 ÷ [ ] = 8

❽ Alice has her birthday in November, and Jane's birthday is four months later. In which month is Jane's birthday?

[ ]

❾ How many 20p coins can I get for £2.00? [ ] 20p coins

❿ If fifteen boys have ten badges each, how many badges do they have altogether? [ ] badges

/10

Practice Page 21

Mixed questions

1. What is $\frac{3}{4}$ of £2.00? £ . p

2. The difference between 125 and 145 is

3. (56 ÷ 8) x 3 =

4. Increase 19 by 31 and double your answer.

5. How many grams are there in 4 kilograms 260 grams? g

6. What is the value of the 5 in this number? 1,562

7. I saved 9 pence a week for eight weeks. How much money do I have? p

8. How many whole ones can I make from six halves? whole ones

9. 80p – 37p = p

10. If each side of this square measures 7 centimetres, what is the length of all the sides put together? cm

/10

Mixed questions

1 **Add $\frac{1}{2}$ metre and 26 centimetres.** ______ **cm**

2 **Add 125 grams to 160 grams.** ______ **g**

3 **How many sevens make 56?** ______ **sevens**

4 ______ **÷ 6 = 9**

5 **A ribbon 56 centimetres long is cut into eight equal pieces. How long is each piece?** ______ **cm**

Write this as a numeral:

6 **three thousand four hundred and seventy-two** ______

7 **There are one hundred and sixty children on a boat. If fifty-five are boys, how many girls are there?**

______ **girls**

8 **Sally has £3.25, and Lisa has three times as much. How much does Lisa have?** **£ ___ . ___ p**

9 **1 metre of sticky tape costs 8 pence. How much will $9\frac{1}{2}$ metres cost?** ______ **p**

10 **150 + 250 =** ______

/10

Practice Page 23

Mixed questions

1. 

If this clock is 25 minutes slow, what time should it show?

2. **£2.50 – 75p =** £ . p

3. **What is the cost of six pencils at 8 pence each?** p

4. **(45 + 25) ÷ 7 =**

5. Put these numbers in order. Start with the smallest.

3,152 3,521 2,531 2,315 5,132 5,213

6. **A kilogram of apples costs 45 pence. How much will 2 kilograms cost?** p

7. Complete this sequence.

1 $1\frac{1}{2}$ 2 ☐ 3 $3\frac{1}{2}$ 4 ☐ ☐ ☐ 6

8. **A 2-metre length of wire is cut into ten equal pieces. How long is each piece?** cm

9. **$1\frac{1}{4} + 2\frac{1}{2} =$**

10. **Subtract six tens from 100.**

/10

Practice Page 24

Mixed questions

1. 9 x 6 = tens units

2. A television programme starts at 8 o'clock and ends 45 minutes later. What time does it end?

3. How many half metres are there in $5\frac{1}{2}$ metres? half m

4. What number is double 500?

5. Increase 28 pence by £2.30. £ . p

6. Share fifty-six sweets equally among eight children. sweets

Underline the odd numbers.

7. 125 146 117 148 153

8. You have £5.00 to spend, but you only spend half of it. How much do you have left? £ . p

9. Toby weighs 24 kilograms, and Joe is 7 kilograms heavier. How heavy is Joe? kg

10. 1,000 + 400 + 20 + 6 =

/10

Practice Page **25**

Mixed questions

❶ 25 ÷ ☐ = 5

❷ ☐ x 6 = 42

❸ 8 x ☐ = 72

❹ (24 ÷ 4) x 8 = ☐

❺ **I buy 1 kilogram of apples, 2 kilograms of potatoes, $\frac{1}{2}$ a kilogram of bananas and 250 grams of grapes. What is their total weight?** ☐

❻ **If I have two £1 coins, three 20p coins and one 10p coin, how much money do I have altogether?** £ . p

❼ **What is the difference between (3 x 7) and (6 x 4)?** ☐

❽ What is the value of the 6 in this number?

6,251 ☐

❾ **How many months are there in two years?** ☐ months

❿ 4 x 25 = ☐

/10

Practice Page 26

Mixed questions

1. (6 + 14) x 5 = ______

2. 72 ÷ 9 = ______

3. 50p + 30p + 10p = ______ p

4. How many months are there in half a year? ______ months

5. What is the product of 7 and 9? ______

6. Divide 450 by 10. ______

7. I hour take away 20 minutes leaves ______ minutes

8. Multiply three by six, and add five. ______

9. Steven bought a hundred and fifty marbles in packets of five. How many packets did he buy? ______ packets

10. How many fifties are there in four hundred and fifty? ______ fifties

/ 10

Practice Page 27

Mixed questions

❶ 25 + 34 = ☐

❷ 8 x ☐ = 56

❸ 81 ÷ ☐ = 9

❹ (100 – 75) x 2 = ☐

Write this number in words:

❺ 6,217 ☐

❻ A film starts at a quarter past 7. If it is $1\frac{3}{4}$ hours long, what time does it end? ☐

❼ John weighs 40 kilograms and Michael weighs 28 kilograms. What is the difference in weight? ☐ kg

Underline the even numbers.

❽ 24 37 56 98 110

❾ I need 14 pence more to give me £6.00. How much money do I have? £ . p

❿ A chocolate bar has eight sections. How many sections are there in thirty bars? ☐ sections

/10

Practice Page 28

Mixed questions

1. What is 25 grams more than 30 grams? ______ g

2. 7,000 + 500 + 60 + 4 = ______

3. 72 ÷ ______ = 8

4. 64p + 33p = ______ p

5. What time does this digital clock show?

______ minutes to ______

6. How many centimetres are there in $3\frac{3}{4}$ metres? ______ cm

7. I can buy a bat and ball for £2.60. If the ball costs 85 pence, how much does the bat cost? £ ______ . ______ p

8. Find the product of 8 and 4, and double it. ______

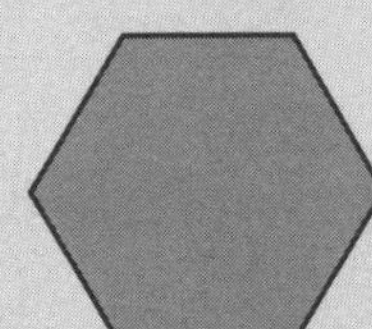

9. If each side of this regular hexagon measures 8 centimetres, what is the length of all the sides put together? ______ cm

10. If ten postcards cost 80 pence, how much will four postcards cost? ______ p

/10

Totaliser

Colour in the squares as you complete each Practice Page to show your score out of ten marks.

Practice Page										
1										
2										
3										
4										
5										
6										
7										
8										
9										
10										
11										
12										
13										
14										
15										
16										
17										
18										
19										
20										
21										
22										
23										
24										
25										
26										
27										
28										

How well did you do?

Answers

PRACTICE PAGE 1

1 < 2 >
3 <
4 3 tens 8 units
5 6 tens 9 units
6 13 24 33 58 62 74
7 43 53 63
8 80 pencils
9 29 10 38

PRACTICE PAGE 2

1 4 2 30
3 10 4 15
5 67 57 47 37
6 60 7 32
8 30 25 20 15 10
9 30 10 16 sweets

PRACTICE PAGE 3

1 8 2 36
3 28 4 20
5 100 6 4
7 eighty-six
8 6 12 15 21 24
9 50 10 24

PRACTICE PAGE 4

1 10 sevens
2 3 lots of nine
3 4 4 3
5 20 6 5
7 3 marbles 8 3
9 8 10 5 cards

PRACTICE PAGE 5

1 semicircle 2 pentagon
3 hexagon 4 4 sides
5 24cm
6 250cm
7 5 metres 8 50cm
9 500g 10 $\frac{1}{2}$ litre

PRACTICE PAGE 6

1 29p 2 45p
3 30p 4 £1.00p
5 £3.00p 6 50p 5p
7 £2.54p 8 75p
9 40p 10 35p

PRACTICE PAGE 7

1 7 o'clock
2 quarter past 4
3 quarter to 7 4 half past 9
5 10.45 6 1.15
7 8.30
8 1 hour 8 minutes
9 75 minutes 10 6 hours

PRACTICE PAGE 8

1 12 2 10
3 23 4 24p
5 10p 6 40cm
7 35g 8 $2\frac{1}{2}$ m
9 £5.00p 10 11th May

PRACTICE PAGE 9

1 355 2 400
3 123 132 213 231 312 321
4 246 264 426 462 624 642
5 353 6 741
7 325 425 525
8 800 9 423
10 345

PRACTICE PAGE 10

1 20 2 415
3 332 4 445
5 60 girls 6 55 marbles
7 180 8 60
9 fifty 10 85 sweets

PRACTICE PAGE 11

1 24 2 8
3 4 4 6
5 4 6 80 books
7 110 stamps
8 60 soft toys
9 £1.00p 10 46p

PRACTICE PAGE 12

1 24 2 30
3 40 4 21
5 36
6 3 biscuits
7 4 packets 8 5
9 15 fives 10 12 bracelets

PRACTICE PAGE 13

1 $\frac{1}{5}$ 2 $\frac{1}{3}$
3 $\frac{1}{10}$
4 10 tenths 5 5 fifths
6 6 7 4
8 4 9 10cm
10 20p

PRACTICE PAGE 14

1 50p 2 5p
3 50p 4 70p
5 4 sweets 6 80p
7 75p 8 £2.00p
9 50p 10 783p

PRACTICE PAGE 15

1 quarter past 10
2 quarter to 7 3 25 to 9
4 2.45 5 4.18
6 8.40 7 12.55
8 75 minutes 9 35 minutes
10 4 hours

PRACTICE PAGE 16

1 four hundred and sixty-three
2 316
3 44 42 40 38
4 5 5 12kg
6 275cm
7

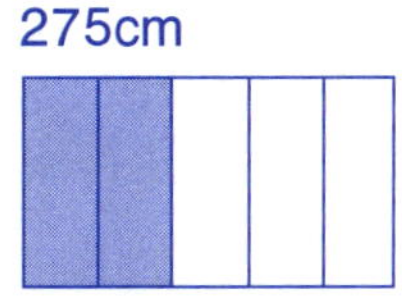

8 180 minutes 9 3.35
10 100

PRACTICE PAGE 17

1 25 — 2 24
3 24 — 4 35
5 24 — 6 34
7 10 — 8 4
9 8 — 10 60

PRACTICE PAGE 18

1 519 — 2 23
3 5p — 4 6m
5 150 — 6 100
7 100 — 8 6 half kg
9 2,000g — 10 30

PRACTICE PAGE 19

1 5 — 2 60
3 12 — 4 2m 24cm
5 60 model animals
6 half past 3 — 7 70cm
8 100g — 9 40
10 368

PRACTICE PAGE 20

1 20 minutes — 2 £1.20p
3 10 — 4 8
5 30 — 6 157
7 6 — 8 March
9 10 20p coins — 10 150 badges

PRACTICE PAGE 21

1 £1.50p — 2 20
3 21 — 4 100
5 4,260g — 6 500
7 72p
8 3 whole ones
9 43p — 10 28cm

PRACTICE PAGE 22

1 76cm — 2 285g
3 8 sevens — 4 54
5 7cm — 5 3,472
7 105 girls — 8 £9.75p
9 76p — 10 400

PRACTICE PAGE 23

1 half past 4 — 2 £1.75p
3 48p — 4 10
5 2,315 2,531 3,152 3,521 5,132 5,213
6 90p
7 $2\frac{1}{2}$ $4\frac{1}{2}$ 5 $5\frac{1}{2}$
8 20cm — 9 $3\frac{3}{4}$
10 40

PRACTICE PAGE 24

1 5 tens 4 units
2 quarter to 9 — 3 11 half m
4 1,000 — 5 £2.58p
6 7 sweets
7 125 146 117 148 153
8 £2.50p — 9 31kg
10 1,426

PRACTICE PAGE 25

1 5 — 2 7
3 9 — 4 48
5 3kg 750g / $3\frac{3}{4}$kg
6 £2.70p — 7 3
8 6,000 — 9 24 months
10 100

PRACTICE PAGE 26

1 100 — 2 8
3 90p — 4 6 months
5 63 — 6 45
7 40 minutes — 8 23
9 30 packets — 10 9 fifties

PRACTICE PAGE 27

1 59 — 2 7
3 9 — 4 50
5 six thousand two hundred and seventeen
6 9 o'clock — 7 12kg
8 24 37 56 98 110
9 £5.86p
10 240 sections

PRACTICE PAGE 28

1 55g — 2 7,564
3 9 — 4 97p
5 10 minutes to 4
6 375cm — 7 £1.75p
8 64 — 9 48cm
10 32p

ISBN 0 340 73672 0

First published in Great Britain 1999

10 9 8 7 6 5 4 3 2 1

Published by Hodder Children's Books, a division of Hodder Headline plc, 338 Euston Road, London NW1 3BH

Printed and bound in Great Britain

A CIP record is registered by and held at the British Library.